Raising the Perfect Dog

The Secrets of Law Enforcement K9 Trainers

Nicholas R. White

CONTENTS

Introduction   v

1. Choosing the Perfect Dog   1

2. Crate Training   7

3. Confidence-Building   15

4. Socialization   23

5. Being the Pack Leader   27

6. The Use of a Verbal Marker for Training   33

7. Teaching the Basic Commands with Verbal Markers   36

8. Pros and Cons of Different Training Methods   47

9. Do's and Don'ts of Training   53

10. Importance of Physical and Mental Exercise   57

11. Troubleshooting Common Problems   63

12. Summary   77

INTRODUCTION

First off, thank you for purchasing my book. I hope you truly feel that the information I am about to give was worth more than the purchase price!

About me: I run one of the most successful dog-training businesses in the state of Virginia. We currently have four training locations and are rapidly growing. My experience started when I was very young, working with our dog Deputy, a German shepherd mix, when I was about 14 years old. I spent every day working with Deputy, teaching him anything and everything I could. From the basics (sit, down, come) to barking on command, rolling over, playing dead, to setting a treat on his nose. Right then, I knew I had found my passion. Fast forward about four years—I joined the U.S. Marine Corps and worked with our military working dogs. Out of the Marine Corps, I was immediately hired by a federal law enforcement agency in Washington, DC, and then worked alongside our apprehension and bomb-detection dogs for more than three years. By this time, I had more than enough skills, experience, training, and knowledge to open my own business, Off-Leash K9 Training. Currently, it is one of the most successful dog-training businesses in the state of Virginia. We currently have four training locations and we're growing. I have spent more than 10 years in trial and error, seminars, schools, and working with hundreds of dogs ranging from household pets to military working dogs to figure out what the best methods were for raising a happy, confident, friendly, and well-trained dog. So this is 10 years of my life, experiences, and knowledge compiled together to bring you the best book on raising a happy, confident, friendly, well-trained dog. You will notice throughout this book I make many analogies comparing dogs to humans; there are so many similarities and behaviors that we have in common that it is almost frightening. I'm sure you too will begin to see some of these in your own dog that you can compare to your children or even yourself. I hope you enjoy reading this book as much as I enjoyed writing it, and I am certain that if you follow the guidance in this book, you will have a happy, confident, friendly, and well-trained dog!

CHOOSING THE PERFECT DOG

In order to raise the perfect dog, you have to pick the perfect dog—that is, the perfect dog for you. Many people ask, "What is the best dog to get?" Unfortunately, I cannot answer that, only you can. The question you should ask yourself is, "What am I looking for in a dog?" Are you looking for a very energetic dog that needs a lot of exercise, attention, and work (German shepherd, Belgian Malinois, Lab, etc)? Or are you looking for just a good dog to have as a companion who is completely happy just lying around the house all day? Or are you looking for something in between? Are you looking for a hunting dog, a protection dog, or just a companion? All of these are questions you have to ask yourself; your answer will help you decide what dog is perfect for *you*. There is no perfect dog. The Belgian Malinois is a very high–energy, high–maintenance dog and therefore is not meant for everyone. Pugs and poodles aren't meant for everyone, either. So it really depends on what you are looking for. Also, look at the expectations you have for a dog, then ensure the dog you pick is capable of meeting them. Meaning, if you want a dog to do protection, do not get a beagle; if you want a dog as a running partner, do not pick a bulldog. There is not one that would be perfect for everyone, but there is a dog that would be perfect for you and what you want.

Once you decide on the dog you want, now you have the task of finding a good breeder for that specific type of dog. You should go to a good, qualified breeder, not who many refer to as a "backyard breeder." These are often people with no knowledge, training, or handling of dogs who just so happened to have two dogs, one got pregnant, and now they are selling the puppies. These puppies can have a wide variety of problems, such as temperament, nerves, aggression, and medical concerns. I always recommend finding someone who is an American Kennel Club (AKC)-certified breeder; meaning, their dogs have been tested and come from good, proven lines, genetically and medically. An AKC breeder should have your puppy's family lineage for at least a few generations back, often further.

If you are against breeders because you think they are just in it for the money, you are mistaken. Often they make very little profit off their dogs after they pay for food, medical care, and shots. Keep in mind, you cannot put a price on the eight weeks of headaches, loss of sleep, and messes made in the house by the litter of pups. I love dogs, however, for the very little profit per dog, it is definitely not worth it for me to take care of six to 12 puppies for eight weeks.

Now that you have some great breeders lined up, ensure the breeder can deliver the specific type of dog you are looking for. A big misconception people have is that if they have a German shepherd, a Belgian Malinois, or a Rottweiler that we can turn him or her into a great protection dog. That is far from the truth. Generally, protection dogs are bought from breeders who breed specifically for this type of work; meaning, they will take two high-drive, high-confidence, good-nerved dogs (usually former protection dogs) and breed them together. Not every dog out of their litter will be successful in this line of work. So, ensure the breeder you are using is breeding for what you are looking for in your dog. If you want a Lab to be used as a hunting dog, ensure you are getting a Lab that is bred from a working line. People breed for families/companions, for looks and show, and for working lines, so you have to ensure the breeder you choose is breeding not only the breed of dog but also the type of dog that you are looking for.

Once you've really narrowed it down to a specific breeder, do your research. Breeders are like any other business in the world, you cannot take their word for it just because it is their business. Ask for references, talk to other people who bought the same type of dog you are looking for and contact them. See if their dog is what they expected, if they had any problems, how their dealings were with the breeder. Remember, getting a dog is around a14-year commitment, so it is important to ensure that you are getting exactly what you want. A good breeder will ask you as many questions as you ask them, so red flags should go up if you can just show up with the money and take their dog without any questions from either side. Generally the breeder will have an application with a questionnaire, they will want to meet with you in advance, and they will want to find out as much about you as possible. Also, they should tell you that their dogs are not available until they are eight weeks old—this is another good indicator to look out for. Up until eight weeks, the puppies are still with their mother, learning to interact with their siblings, learning vital things such as bite inhibition (what is acceptable and unacceptable play, etc.). Great breeders want to ensure their dogs are going to great homes.

I realize that many dogs are bought from shelters and rescue organizations, so maybe you are thinking that none of this guidance applies to you. Believe it or not, it still applies, just in a different way. If you want to purchase a dog and you do not want to get it from a breeder nor pay the high price that often comes with many purebred dogs, then a dog shelter or a rescue organization is a great way to go. As I stated earlier, do not get a dog from a backyard breeder—someone who is in it only for the money and does not care about the dog's health or well-being. Remember, often they are having a litter in the first place due to their negligence and irresponsibility. So go to a shelter or a rescue organization. These people truly care about dogs and want to ensure their dogs have a good home. Once you find a good, reputable, nonprofit shelter or rescue organization, you can apply the same guidance for picking a happy, confident, and friendly dog.

Now that you have found a great breeder or shelter, you need to pick the perfect pup from that litter. No matter what any breeder tells you, you cannot pick a pup that is right for you online or through a photo. Actually go to their location and choose a dog, even if it's out of state. If you talk to anyone who has picked pups out of a litter, they will usually tell you the pup picked them. I am not saying you will get a horrible dog if you pick one online, I am just saying you will feel much more comfortable and confident about your choice if you go see them in person. Generally, at eight weeks, you can tell a lot about the pup. If they are shy, skittish, and hanging out away from everyone in the litter at eight weeks, there is a great chance that's how they will be when they are older. However, if they are confident, very open and affectionate, and love to play tug at eight weeks, there is a great chance that's how they will be when they are older. These are things you would know only by actually going and observing the litter for yourself. Then, based on what you are looking for, you can pick the pup that you think best suits your needs.

When picking dogs for personal protection, we use a breeder who breeds specifically for that type of work, as I stated above. Once we identify a reputable breeder, we go to their location and put their litter of puppies through a series of tests. Even if you are just looking for a regular household pet, this is still a great test to ensure your dog has an overall good temperament. First, you do not want a puppy who is away from the litter; meaning, off by itself and not socializing or playing with the others. We are looking for the puppies jumping at their gate in order to great us; this shows they are happy to socialize with people. Second, we will test their "drive," in other words, how motivated are they to go after something? We are looking for dogs that have a great prey drive, so when we roll a ball, we want a puppy that will chase after it and preferably bring it back. This shows they have a high drive, which is essential. Additionally, we are looking for that same level of motivation when they play tug; for protection, your dog must have a great tug drive. As we go through these steps, we are slowly eliminating the pups that do not have these characteristics.

For their second phase of testing, we will take one-on-one the pups who have passed the prior steps in order to evaluate them further. One of the things we do is get them really excited by playing with them and then rolling them over to their backs to see how easily they submit. Ideally, you want a puppy that is fighting to get up. This shows they are not very quick to submit. We follow that with a drop test, which involves us playing with the pup and then dropping something loud beside it or making a loud noise (dropping a metal bowl, a loud clap, etc.). Ideally, you are looking for a puppy that does not overreact to a loud noise. If they do overreact, we are looking for a quick recovery, meaning, you can quickly get them to come back and engage them back into the play. One of the final things we do is the pinch test. While playing with the dog, we give them a pinch on the side until they give a little whimper. This is done to test their ability to forgive the handler for giving them a correction, meaning, how they react when the handler gives them an unpleasant feeling. Do they shut down and run away or do they quickly forgive and come back? We are looking for a puppy that does not immediately run away from us. For those that do run away, we want one that we can quickly get to come back.

If you are getting a dog from a shelter or rescue organization, add in the additional step of taking the dog out and around other dogs, people, and kids in order to see how they behave with them. This is done to ensure you are not getting a people- or dog-aggressive dog before you take him home. Often, people get a dog from a shelter or rescue organization and a week later they have their first encounter with another dog or child and find their dog is aggressive. An additional step you may want to take is seeing how the dog from the shelter is with food and toys. While the dog is eating and playing with toys, touch the dog, the food, and the toy to determine if there is any possible food or toy aggression. Be proactive and find all of this out before you choose a dog.

This is the basic guideline we use in order to find a good, well-balanced, good-tempered, happy, and friendly dog. Just to clarify, there are no guarantees in dogs, however, we have found that this is a great process to follow and it is generally very accurate when trying to predict how a dog will be as it gets older. Then, once you find this perfect dog, follow the guidance in the rest of the book to continuously build on its level of confidence, drive, socialization, and happiness.

CRATE TRAINING

First off, congratulations on your new perfect puppy! Many people do not realize how much work some puppies can be for the first six months of their lives, and that's just the beginning. Essentially, it is like having a newborn baby in many ways as you may have already figured out. Puppies require constant attention and, just like babies, are more than likely waking you up in the middle of the night.

In general, with proper crate training, your puppy should be almost completely housebroken by the age of four to five months. This age can vary depending on how effective you are throughout this process. Remember, your dog does not decide how long it takes to be house-trained, *you* do.

You are probably wondering, "Where do I start?" First, get a crate, preferably one with a divider so you can expand the living space for your pup as it grows. It is nearly impossible to house-train a puppy without using a crate. Housebreaking a puppy is based entirely on the crate-training system. Crate training teaches a puppy the crate is *its* spot to go; it's the equivalent of its home. More important, it becomes a location to hold your puppy during the housebreaking process when he cannot be directly supervised.

Pick a crate big enough for your dog to lie down, stand up (without his or her back touching the top of the cage), and spin around in a circle. Do not put a small puppy inside a large crate. They should have not have much more room than described above. I always recommend getting a large crate that has the adjustable divider in it. This way, you only need to buy one crate and can adjust the space as your puppy grows. If you find your puppy is going to the restroom inside the crate, you may want to reduce the size of the space. Often, if the crate is too large in relation to the size of your puppy, he does not have a problem going in the back corner of the crate because he can get far enough away from the mess that it doesn't affect him as much.

Your puppy should be in its crate a lot for the first couple of months it is home with you. Don't feel bad about keeping him in the crate. To put it into perspective, a crib is simply a crate for babies. You put babies in their cribs to protect them from themselves. A puppy should be looked at the same way.

Take the initiative with your puppy. As a general rule, your puppy will have to go outside approximately 30 minutes after eating or drinking. So if you know he just ate or drank a lot of water, take the initiative and take him out; do not wait for him to go in the house. Also, it is a good idea to take him out after a good play session in the house. If you are playing tug, chasing the ball, or getting the puppy really excited, it is always a good idea to take the initiative and take him out after these sessions, as well.

Using a keyword phrase during housebreaking is very important. From the first day you get your puppy, start to implement a keyword while your puppy is going to the restroom outside. Most people prefer the phrase "go potty." So any time your pup is sniffing in the grass when you take him outside, repeat the key phrase "go potty." As soon as your pup uses the restroom, immediately praise him (verbally, physically, and/or with a treat). Over time, he will associate the key phrase "go potty" with the act of going to the restroom, about a month into the housebreaking process. After this period, if you see your pup start to display that he is going to go to the restroom in the house (tail up, sniffing around in circles, etc.), repeat that phrase he has been hearing from day one, "Do you have to go potty?" He will recognize that key phrase he has associated with going outside and will run to the door, indicating that he does indeed have to go out. This is the first step of progress for housebreaking.

Use a bell on a string to teach your puppy to let you know that he has to go outside. Tie a bell to the end of a string and hang it from the doorknob at approximately your pup's chest level. Every time you take your pup outside, ring the bell with his paw. Praise him immediately and open the door. Doing this every time you go out teaches the dog that ringing the bell equals the door opening. Over a period of time, your pup will learn: "If I have to go outside to the restroom, I ring bell and the door opens."

The most important thing to effectively housebreak your puppy is total supervision. I will state it again, because it is *that* important: *total supervision.*.What does that mean? Simple; it means if your puppy is not inside its crate, you or another member of the household should be directly supervising him. Until the pup is completely housebroken, there should *never* come a time when he is in a room alone. To put it into perspective, if you are downstairs with your puppy and decide to take a shower, even if it is just five minutes, put your pup inside its crate. Again, think of your pup as a baby. If you have a baby and you are going to jump in the shower or leave the room to fold laundry, would you leave a baby just sitting in the living room by itself? No, you would put it in the crib. Again, a crib is simply a crate for babies.

If, while supervising your pup, you see him squat and start peeing or pooping, immediately give a loud verbal, "No!" Pick him up, immediately take him outside, and set him down in the yard. Then repeat that key phrase, "Go potty." As soon as he finishes, give praise (verbal, physical, and/or a treat) and take him back inside. There should *never* be any punishment involved. Rubbing his nose in it, hitting him, rolling a newspaper—these are all things that are proven ineffective. More important, it just breaks down the bond between you and your pup. Physically punishing a puppy for going to the restroom in the house is like spanking a one-year-old for going in their diaper.

Many people ask, "What if I didn't catch him in the act, but noticed he went to the restroom in the house?" Very simple, do absolutely nothing. That's right, do absolutely nothing. Write it off as a failure on *your* part, clean it up, and move on. Again, do not punish the puppy. *You* failed him, he did not fail you. You violated the biggest rule in housebreaking: You failed to give him total supervision. This is so important it is worth mentioning once more: If you do not physically catch your dog in the act, chalk it up to a loss on your behalf and move on. Make it your goal to catch him every single time. For every time your pup goes in the house without being caught in the act, you add a few more days to the housebreaking process. So, if he is going in the house a couple times per day without getting caught in the act, the housebreaking process can be *really* prolonged..

Your puppy should sleep in the crate every night when you go to bed (again, because if you are sleeping, you cannot directly supervise him). When you first wake up in the morning, take him from the crate straight outside and use the key phrase ("Go potty"). If your puppy does not go to the restroom, take him back in the house and put him back into the crate. Approximately 15 to 20 minutes later. take him out of the crate, back outside, and repeat the process. Repeat this until your puppy *does* go to the restroom outside. This does two things: It prevents him from coming back in and minutes later going to the restroom in your house and will teach your puppy that he has to go to the restroom or he will keep going back into the crate until he does. After a few days of this, he will just go outside the first time you take him out. After he goes to the restroom outside, bring him back into your house and leave him out of the crate, remembering to directly supervise him.

We recommend that you do not put padding in the crate until the pup is housebroken and more mature. We feel this is important for a couple of reasons. Most important, if you are gone, your puppy will more than likely chew, shred, or eat this padding/bedding at some point, which can become a choking hazard for a small puppy. Additionally, often puppies who have padding in the crate will still urinate in their crate because the padding acts as a sponge and absorbs the urine. Therefore, it does not bother them to urinate there; the padding acts as a diaper.

What about puppy pads? I think puppy pads are a bad idea, especially if you have a puppy that will grow into a large dog. Puppy pads teach the puppy it's okay to go to the restroom in the house, however, only in this specific area. I find it much easier to teach them it's never acceptable to go to the restroom in the house. Additionally, as the pup grows into a larger dog, do you really want them going to the restroom *inside your house?* They may go in a specific spot, however, the smell usually permeates the whole house.

Another important thing to remember is to *never* let your dog out of the crate if he is actively barking or whining. This will teach your dog that if he barks and whines long enough, you will let him out. It is like the child who throws a fit in the middle of the toy store, and then the parents buy the kid a toy. The child simply learns that if he makes a big enough scene, he will get his way. Dogs learn the same way. So never let your dog out of the crate if he is actively barking or whining. Doing so rewards bad behavior. Your pup should learn that he gets out of the crate only when he is quiet. Just to clarify, your new puppy may whine in the middle of the night to let you know he has to go out. It is then acceptable to let him out of the crate, take him outside, use the key phrase, then come back in. However, once your puppy is old enough to hold it throughout the night (generally around three to four months of age), never let him out based on whining or barking.

During the housebreaking process, we usually recommend cutting off food and water around 7 p.m. This is done to ensure that all of the water has passed through the pup's system by the time you go to sleep (assuming you are going to bed around 9 p.m. or later). If you cut off food and water at around 7 p.m., it will minimize having to go in the middle of the night. Additionally, do not put food or water in the crate with the pup; again, this will cause him to have to go to the restroom in the middle of the night.

Never use the crate as a place to punish your puppy, as hard as it sometimes may be. If you start using the crate as a place of punishment, the pup will start to hate it, will not want to go in, and will no longer see it as its "home." Rather, he will see at is a prison. The crate should always be looked upon as something positive. The crate should be seen by the dog, as you see your bedroom, as a place to go, get away, and relax. It is also a good practice to feed him in the crate or give him a treat every time he goes in, again, associating it with something positive.

If you follow all these principles, you should have a very short housebreaking process and a dog that loves going into the crate.

CONFIDENCE-BUILDING

Anytime we do puppy consultations for new dog owners, one of the main things I discuss is confidence-building. To me, that is one of the most important things in getting a new dog. If you have a highly confident and well-socialized dog, the rest is easy. We will talk more in depth about socialization in the next chapter. Many people think that dogs who bite people are highly confident, and that's why they bite. In fact, it's quite the opposite; generally, they have very low confidence and are not well socialized. A confident dog knows you are not a challenge or a threat, so there's no reason to try to "show you." That's why a lot of the smaller dogs bark at people more than the bigger dogs do. Generally, the best fighters do not cause many problems. There is a reason you do not see people like UFC star Rich Franklin in the news for getting into fights outside the octagon. Because he is confident, he does not need to prove himself to anyone. The same thing applies to police, military, and personal-protection dogs. Most of their training revolves around confidence-building. Also, that is why you almost never see in the news that a police, military, or personal-protection dog mauls a child to death. That is because they are well socialized, highly confident, and they know that child does not pose any threat to them. Unfortunately, you see it in the news all too often with regular house pets, because of, again, a lack of confidence and socialization.

So, what are some things you can do to ensure your puppy is highly confident? Assuming you got your dog from a reputable breeder, as discussed earlier, you can use the numerous drills we use with our protection dogs to make them highly confident.

As soon as you get your puppy, start immediately exposing him to as many noises as possible. Turn on the vacuum, blender, hair dryer, and any other noisy devices you have around the house. I have seen far too many dogs that run and hide at the sound of a loud noise, especially vacuum cleaners and thunder. This can be completely prevented if you expose them to these noises at a young age. Expose your dog to as many noises as possible by the time he is five months old, and while exposing him, make it a positive experience through verbal/physical praise, treats, etc.

What to do if you expose your puppy to a noise (e.g., a vacuum) and he runs and hides from it? Very simple—bring him back and make him deal with it. One of the many terms we use for this process is "flooding." This means you find a noise your dog is afraid of and flood him with that noise repeatedly, every day. Again, flood him with this experience in a positive way, by giving praise, treats, etc. Fear of noises or things is a completely unrealistic fear that dogs have, just like humans. So, by making him sit next to the vacuum cleaner while it's turned on, he realizes, "I'm not being hurt, I don't feel any pain, and I am getting praised for this." After a short while, that unrealistic fear will go away and the dog will soon realize that it is not a big deal and will soon pay no attention to it.

What if my puppy hears a lot of noise such as thunder, fireworks, or a car door slam outside and he runs to me for comfort? Never comfort your dog when he is afraid of something. This only reinforces the fear. Comfort is simply another kind of praise. Think about that for a second. When you comfort a dog, how is it different from praising him? You are petting them and talking cute to them in both instances. So when you break it down, you are praising your dog for being afraid of something. Now, any time it has a reason to be afraid, it will run to you in order to reap the praise that goes along with the action. So, never comfort your dog for being afraid. If he hears a loud noise and comes running to you, do not acknowledge him, do not look at him, touch him, pet him, or talk to him. Again, if he sees it does not get a response from you and you do not make a big deal out of it, he will not make a big deal out of it, either.

What if I expose my dog to an object that he is afraid of? Same thing—flooding. Flood him with that object in a positive manner. For some odd reason, we get a lot of dogs that are afraid of the pop a trashcan liner makes when the owner shakes it out to open it. I recommend the same process as we do with noises. Put the dog on a leash, hold him, and just keep popping the trashcan liner over and over. Soon enough, he will not even acknowledge it. Also, if he is afraid of the liner itself, put the liner on your hand and pet him with it. Again, he will soon realize that it is not that bad, it is not hurting him, and he is getting praised.

Often, if you bring a new object into the house, the puppy will run from it, bark at it, etc. Use the same concepts as above—put him on a leash, pull him over to the object, and make him deal with it. Generally, this process will last about 10 minutes or less, and then he will no longer pay attention to the object because he has now faced his fears.

Another important step for confidence-building in a puppy is get him on as many objects, surfaces, textures, and elevations as possible. There are many dogs we train that are afraid to get up on new objects. This is a direct result of underexposure to new objects at a young age. In order to prevent this, put your puppy on as many different things as possible. Set him on chairs, picnic tables, grass, asphalt, dog beds, staircases, wood, concrete, Tupperware containers, tree stumps, park benches, and anything else you can find. The key is (on the lower objects) to put him on there, praise him while he is up there, and then make him get off the object by himself. Again, you are taking away that unrealistic fear by teaching him, "I got up here and was praised. I got off on my own and I'm fine." We put dogs in completely unrealistic situations such as a baby pool filled with empty water bottles. We create situations they are very unlikely to encounter in a real-world situation. Why do it if they would never have to go into a baby pool filled with water bottles? Simple, if they get used to being in absurd surfaces and environments, then realistic things are no problem whatsoever and they do not even think twice about getting on those surfaces.

One of the most important steps to raising a confident dog is to *play tug with your dog.* People do not realize how important this step is in confidence-building. It does not help that there is so much misinformation out there on this subject that people really do not know what to think. In order to get our protection dog very tug-driven, meaning they go crazy when they see the tug and will do anything for it is by limiting their exposure to it. In the Secret Service, our dogs were working for a ball. As soon as the handlers pull that ball out, the dogs go crazy for it by spinning, barking, etc. So, many people would ask, "How do I get my dog that motivated for a ball?" First off, it goes back to breeding and genetics, some dogs from day one just have no interest in tugging or chasing a ball. That is why it is important to know what type of puppy you are getting and who you are getting it from to ensure that the puppy will be able to meet the expectations you have for it.

In order to make your pup highly motivated for a ball, tug, or toy, it is essential that he does not have full access to it. Meaning, he should have only very limited access to that specific toy. If he has access to the ball or tug all throughout the day, he will never be highly motivated for it. Again, a toy to dogs is like money is to you: If you had unlimited access to money, you wouldn't be very motivated to go to work because there is no incentive. The same principles apply with your puppy, if he has constant access to a toy; there is no incentive for him to "work" for it. A dog will never be too motivated for something he always has, just like people. The ball or tug becomes a new treat; they get it only limitedly and on special occasions. If you fed your dog hot dogs every day, three meals per day, for one year, they would no longer be considered a treat to him—it is now food. So think about the ball or tug the same way—limited accessibility and only when they do something deserving.

Generally, we will give dogs the toy or play tug with them only when they are doing something good. When we are training with them, we will do some obedience training, then "mark" the behavior (more on this in the training section) and immediately reward with a quick game of a tug or by throwing the ball for them to chase. As soon as we play tug for a minute or two, we will immediately take the tug back and repeat the training. If we are using the ball, they have it long enough to go get it and bring it back, that's about it. If the pup gets the ball and lies down with it, we immediately take it away. Remember, these are not used as chew toys.

One thing to keep in mind is you do not want to over-train with the tug or the ball. Meaning, you do not want to keep playing with the dog until he loses interest in the tug/ball. Stop playing when the dog still wants to keep going. That is what builds up the drive for it. So, when your pup is still in the prime of wanting to play, we will tease them with the ball or tug and once they get all excited over it, we will simply turn and put it away to end the session. This really helps build their drive. That way, when you go to pull the tug/ball out the next time, they immediately want it and want to play. By repeating this sequence over a period of weeks, you should really see your dog's drive building up for these devices.

Let me correct some misinformation about playing tug with your dog. The first myth is that playing tug with your dog can lead to aggression. That is completely false; actually, the opposite is true. Playing tug has never led to aggression in any dog I have ever seen or worked with. Again, playing tug builds confidence. As I stated in the beginning of this chapter, confident dogs are not the ones biting.

Second myth: You should always win if you play tug in order to show that you are the alpha-male, the dominant member of the pack. Also completely false. Beating your puppy in tug is not something that will teach your dog that you are the leader. What it *will* do is give your puppy low confidence. Think about it—imagine if you and I were to play a game of pool at my house every day after work and I always beat you. How confident would you be in playing pool? Imagine if my friends came over and they always beat you, too. Where would you be on the confidence scale of 1 to 10? That is where your puppy's confidence would be, as well. Now, think of the same scenario but reverse the roles. Now imagine that you always beat me, every one of my friends, and all of my family members. How high would you be on the confidence scale then? In your mind, you are unbeatable. Losing isn't even an option, right?

Welcome to the world of how police, military, and personal protection dogs think. Your pup should always win in the game of tug!

When you start playing tug with your puppy, make it fun, engaging, and exciting. You should get into it as much as he does, if not more. While playing tug with your pup, pet him, lightly tapping him on his sides, head, and chest as he tugs. If you scare him off, encourage him back on, repeat the same process, but just don't do it as much or as hard. This gets your puppy in the habit of being touched while he is tugging and he will become immune to the contact. This is good for when he gets older and possibly works a bite sleeve. Even if that is not your intention for your dog, it is still good to do this drill in order to build confidence while playing tug.

Next, we start incorporating noise desensitization while playing tug with your puppy. Earlier, we talked about desensitizing them to noises in general, now we are going to apply those same concepts to desensitizing them while playing tug. Start small with something such as two spoons that you bang together as you play tug. Again, if the puppy gets scared and backs off the tug, encourage him back on, then make the same noises but not as loud. Then start to build the noise back up. Once he gets used to this, find something louder, such as banging on a saucepan with a metal spoon as you play tug. Again, if he comes off, encourage back on, and make the noise quieter, then build it back up. Once he adapts, find something even louder, and then repeat this process over and over. This is how we build dogs up to the point that they bite on a sleeve and we can shoot a gun over their head and they do not even flinch. Again, this is huge for their confidence.

Another good thing for confidence is praising the dog for barking when someone is at the door. When your puppy gets to be four or five months old, he may run to the door and bark when someone knocks. Some people take the unfortunate step of quickly telling their dog to be quiet or yelling at him. Remember, you got a big dog for a form of protection around the house, even if it was just to put on a good show for a would-be robber. So, I tell everyone they should praise their pup for this behavior. If you always quickly stop them or quiet them down, they will do exactly as you wish—eventually, they will never make a noise if someone is breaking in because every time they tried to give you a verbal warning that someone was outside, you quickly shut them up. Remember, dogs aim to please, so if you always stop your dog from barking at the sound of someone outside, he will do just that—never bark.

The key is to praise the behavior, but be able to silence them on command when you wish. We always let our protection dogs bark for a few seconds, praise them, and then give them the "quiet" command. That way, you are getting the best of both worlds. You have a dog that is alert, gets his confidence up by being praised when he gives you a verbal warning, and you can control it so it is not over the top or annoying. The key is you do not want to teach them not to bark, you want to be able to control their barking.

If you follow all these steps, you will have a highly confident pup that is comfortable in any situation.

SOCIALIZATION

What is socialization? It is getting your puppy acquainted with as many different animals, people, and circumstances as possible. In my opinion, socialization is one of the most important things in young puppies' lives. If I were paid every time we received e-mails or calls about people-aggressive or dog-aggressive dogs, I could have retired by now. Almost all of these cases stem from a lack of socialization at a young age. When you get any new puppy, it is extremely important to get him to start interacting with other animals and people.

To get your dog well socialized with people, try having everyone your puppy meets give him a treat. Imagine if everyone you met gave you $50. You would quickly grow very fond of people; your puppy will, too. Your pup will start making the association of "people equal great things for me." You should make it your mission for your puppy to meet as many people and animals as possible. Not only as many people as possible, but as many types of people as possible—male, female, children, infants, and even different races. He should have complete exposure to as many variations of humans as possible.

Socializing your puppy with other dogs and animals is also extremely important. Again, most cases of aggression result from a lack of socialization. As I write this paragraph, there is a dog in our facility on its first lesson who is extremely people-aggressive. When I asked the owner how the dog got that way, he replied, "We never really had him around anyone other than our family." With this particular Lab, you cannot even touch him without him trying to bite you. This is why socialization is so important. This should be something you start doing almost immediately after you bring your puppy home. This teaches him to properly interact with other dogs at an early age. Ensure you are socializing your dog with other dogs that are very friendly. Initially, we recommend this socialization should be with only a few dogs at a time. Also, it should be supervised to ensure it stays safe play.

Do not take your puppy to dog parks for socialization. Yes, you read this correctly, dog parks are a bad idea in my opinion. Again, we receive many e-mails from people whose dogs are now aggressive toward other dogs after being bitten at a dog park. People do not realize that this happens all the time, and they just do not hear about it. Only attacks on people make the news, not attacks on other dogs. The dogs at dog parks come from a wide variety of backgrounds and their owners often know very little about their own dog. Unlike a doggy day-care, in a dog-park environment, there are no trained supervisors walking around, ensuring the play is safe. Also, no evaluations are done in order to accept the dogs into the dog park. Essentially, you are taking a big gamble by exposing your dog to other dogs you know nothing about.

Usually, the dogs in dog parks are of various sizes, backgrounds, and levels of training. Essentially, they are a pack of dogs. Dogs usually consider themselves a pack when there are four or more dogs present. As you know, any time there is a pack, there *has* to be a pack leader. In order for a dog to become the pack leader, he has to assert his force onto other dogs to show them he is in charge of the pack. The end result is a dog getting bitten. Now, your dog that you have done so great with is now dog-aggressive because he was bitten by another dog at a dog park, and now he associates dogs with being harmed.

There are numerous other ways to socialize your dog without the use of a dog park, such as taking them to a doggy day-care. As I mentioned above, doggy day-cares evaluate dogs before admitting them into their facility, drastically reducing the chances of a dominant dog being there. Additionally, they have trained personnel constantly monitoring the dogs' behaviors. In the event that a dog does start displaying any dominant characteristics, they are immediately corrected or separated from the group. Another good way to socialize is one-on-one with other known dog-friendly dogs. Or take them to a pet store on the weekends so they can interact with other dogs and people.

A big misconception many people have is something along the lines of "I want my dog to protect my family; I don't want him to be friendly with everyone." Unfortunately, most people don't know that socialization and a protection dog have absolutely nothing in common. In fact, almost all trained protection dogs are extensively socialized. They love people, kids, animals, and other dogs. They are friendly with everyone, and are taught to bite only a specific individual on command. An under-socialized and low-confidence dog is more prone to bite a person at random (a family member, child, neighbor, etc.).

Regardless of what your goals are with your new dog—show, protection, detection, search and rescue, or just a regular household pet—socialization is one of the most important things you can do with a new puppy. A well-socialized dog is a much more confident dog, as well. It is confident around all people and animals. This is an essential step to ensure you have a happy, confident and well-trained dog.

BEING THE PACK LEADER

What does it mean that dogs are pack animals? This means they always roam and stick together in a pack. Lions are the same way; you will very rarely see a lone lion because they travel in packs. Anytime you have a pack, there has to be a leader in charge of the pack. Think about a pack of dogs like a small business in America. There is no successful business that does not have someone in charge of it. There has to be someone in charge in order to make the decisions, ensure the employees are taken care of and have everything they need, reprimand an employee when he or she does something that goes against the policy of the company, and ensure the overall success of the business. The pack leader, or "alpha-male," of a dog pack essentially has those same responsibilities.

It is imperative that you become the pack leader in your household with the addition of the new member of *your* pack (i.e., your puppy). It is important that you teach your new puppy that you are the pack leader. You must teach him that you are the one who is in charge of the pack; you make the decisions; you have the best of everything; you decide when to play with him; and out of your entire family, you must demonstrate to him that he is the lowest member of the "pack."

Many people wonder why this is important. This is another very important process to ensure that you have a happy, confident, and well-trained dog. Dogs are much happier and stable when they know their place in a pack, and there is no question about who is the dominant individual in the house. As some of you may have already experienced by having dogs, people often say, "My dog listens to my husband really well and does not listen to me at all." Or "My dog will listen to my husband and me, but he will not listen to the kids." Again, this is because your dog knows whom the pack leader is, and listens to him or her. Generally, the person the dog listens to the best is the one who has displayed the best pack leader characteristics and he knows that person is in charge. We are going to discuss many things you can do in order to show your dog you are the pack leader.

One of the most basic things that I always stress to people during their puppy consultations is: Do not let your dog get on the furniture. This is something a lot of people do not like to hear. However, this can and often does lead to major problems in the future. One of the problems with letting your dog get on the furniture is you are bringing them to your level. Essentially, you are teaching them they are on the same level as you and your family. Remember, dogs should be treated as the lowest members of the pack, not as equals. Having them sleep on the floor and on their dog beds is just one more thing to reinforce to them that they are lower members of the pack. Hence, they get the lowest and worst spots to sleep and lie.

Another problem that can be caused with letting them get on the furniture is territorial aggression. I have talked to many clients who tell me that if they try to get their dog off of the couch, he will growl and snap at them—again, because now the dog sees this as an invasion of *his* space. I have talked with numerous people who tell me that when they try to get into bed with their significant other, their dog will growl at them. Again, by bringing them to your level, you can create numerous problems with the order of your pack. You are demonstrating to your dog that he is equal to you; this can lead to many problems.

You should be the first one to do everything. What exactly does that mean, you ask? You should be the first one to eat, then you feed the dog. You should be the first one greeted when a family member arrives home, or if you arrive home first, the family members should be greeted and then the dog. Again, you are reinforcing to him that every member of the family is higher on the pack structure than he is. You should be the first one out the door and the first one up or down the stairs. Simply put your dog in the sit position and then allow him to come after you have gone, or hold him back so he cannot pass you. While walking on the leash, your pup should walk beside you, not in front. Again, leaders walk in the front of the pack. Just keep in mind when you start to work with your dog that you and your family should be the first ones to do everything. The dog always comes last.

In military and law enforcement, generally, our dogs do not have any toys that belong to them. This is done for two reasons, one of which I discussed earlier: Your dog will never be motivated for something to which he has constant access. The second reason we do this is to show the dog that he owns nothing; all toys are ours, and he plays with them when we allow him to. He gets them for doing something good, the toy becomes the treat. Many dogs become toy-aggressive because they have learned that the toys are theirs and you are trying to take their toy. Again, you are the leader, so you control everything in the house. Just like my father was our pack leader, so he controlled the remote control, and he only let us have access to it when he wanted to. Just one more small thing of the many that reaffirmed he was indeed the leader of our household. Get in the habit of touching and playing with your dog while he is eating, or has a bone or a toy. This is done to desensitize them to any possession issues that could arise in the future. Again, they learn that you give the food, toy, bone, or ball, and that you can take it away; it is yours and you are just letting them temporarily have it.

Another important thing about which I get asked about is when dogs try to force their owners to play with them or pet them. For example, you are sitting on the couch and your dog comes over and drops his ball in your lap or lifts up your hand to make you pet him. Those are both examples of your dog trying to make you interact. As hard as it may be, never give in to this forced interaction. Once you give in, your dog will always try to force you to interact. If our dogs do this, we simply pay no attention to them. They learn that their efforts did not pay off and they will no longer try to engage. If you feel you must give your dog a toy, and he keeps dropping it in your lap or next to you, simply put away the toy. This shows them that by trying to force you to play, they lost their toy. Again, they will stop doing this because they will equate this action with getting their toy taken. We teach the dogs that *we* decide when it's time to play, not them.

Never feed your dogs from the table. This is a common mistake. If you do this, you will have a dog that begs, drools, and stalks you and your family at the table. By handing them food from the table, you are teaching your dog that the table is a great source for amazing food. Imagine if every time you hung around the table, your father offered up $100. How much would you be waiting at the table? Your dog has the same mindset as you. If you feel compelled to give your dog table food, wait until everyone from the family has finished and gotten up from the table. Then you can place some of the leftovers in your dog's bowl. By doing so, you are teaching that food never comes from the table and it will only come from his bowl.

Make your dog listen. I always tell our clients, "Never give your dog a command that you are not going to reinforce." That is one of the most important things when it comes to advanced training. If you give a dog a command that you know he knows, you must follow through with it and make him do it, with no exceptions. If you tell him to sit, down, or come, you must ensure he does it, even if you have to physically make him do it. Your dog must learn that once you issue a command, there is no way out of it. Just like with kids, if you let them get away with not doing something you told them to do once, they will try to get out of it the next 10 times. I always tell my clients, "You will never hear me tell a dog something that he doesn't end up doing. Once I say a command, it's not *if* he will do it, but whether they do it on their own. Otherwise I will make him do it." To me, this is an essential principal in training and being the pack leader. If my father told me to clean my room, it was getting done and there was no way out of it and I knew that, so I rarely even tried to get out of it. Apply those same principles to training your dog—if you cannot back it up, don't give the command.

THE USE OF A VERBAL
MARKER FOR TRAINING

First off, if you have purchased a little $3 or $4 device that makes a little click when you press a button, you have fallen for one of the biggest marketing scams that is sweeping dog training worldwide. What the clicker does is give the dog a distinct click to mark the behavior that he just successfully performed. Does it work? Yes, it definitely works in expediting the dog's learning process and drastically cuts down on the time it will take your dog to learn a new command.

If it works, and it works well, why is it a scam? It is a scam because the inventors of the clicker took an old dog-training secret and turned it into a way to make money. We use what we refer to as "marker training." A clicker marks the behavior with a distinct click. Marker training marks the behavior with a verbal command. The marker word I use is "Yes" (said excitedly). Why is marker training better than clicker training? To be honest, clicker training has no advantages whatsoever over a verbal marker. The clicker trainer does have many shortfalls to it, though. Some of the shortfalls to clicker training is that you have to carry this little plastic device everywhere you go in order to mark the behavior, another shortfall is that they are small, so if you lose it, you have to buy another one. The biggest shortfall of the clicker (in my opinion) is that it's something else you have to hold in your hand while trying to teach the dog something, while also holding a treat in your other hand. It can become very complicated to juggle everything at once. The verbal marker training is free, you can do it anywhere, and you never have to fumble with anything extra.

How does marker training work? It works exactly the same as clicker training. First, let me explain how clicker training works. First you must charge the verbal marker. Start by getting your dog to associate getting a treat every time he hears your verbal marker (we will use the word "yes"). So, in order to teach your dog that the word "yes" means something good, start by saying the dog's name. When he looks at you, immediately say yes (excitedly) and give a treat. Repeat this drill. The treat should come immediately after the verbal command is given— literally after one second or less. Tell the dog to sit (assuming he knows the sit command). As soon as his bottom hits the floor, say "yes" and immediately give the treat. Remember, use small pieces of treats when doing the training, that way, your dog will not fill up as fast and will be more motivated to perform for a longer period of time. Also, it helps if you do these training sessions before your dog has eaten, increasing motivation for the food reward. If he knows more commands, give those commands, and say "yes" and immediately give another treat each time a command is obeyed. This is what we call "charging the marker." This gets the dog in the routine of knowing that the word "yes" means something good is immediately going to follow it.

Once you start expanding and go on to teach your dog new tricks that you have learned in books, on television or the Internet, start applying the verbal marker when teaching new tricks. It will vastly decrease the time it takes to learn the new command. If you want to teach your dog to down (lie down), when he does it on his own, mark with a "yes," then immediately give a treat. Your dog learns, "Whatever I did right then is exactly what was wanted of me." That is how it really expedites their learning process.

Marker training is a very fast, easy, effective, and cheap way to train your dog in obedience and you can teach them some pretty neat tricks. When using marker and treat training, be as creative as possible when it comes to thinking of new things to teach the dog. Remember, a bored dog is a destructive dog; this is a great way to keep him entertained. You would be amazed at the number of things they can learn using this training method.

TEACHING THE BASIC COMMANDS WITH VERBAL MARKERS

Teaching the "Come" Command

1. First, find a high-valued treat. A high-valued treat is simply something that your dog really loves. To give you a good hint, most dogs love hot dogs. I always use the chicken or turkey hot dogs just because they are healthier.

2. Create a distraction-free environment for your dog (no TV, no kids running around, no other pets around, etc.). Start charging your marker as described earlier. Say your dog's name. When he looks at you, give the verbal marker "yes" and immediately give a treat. This will help get your dog in training mode.

3. Walk a little bit away from your dog, bend over, and have a treat in your hand at your dog's eye level.

4. Call your dog's name, and follow it by the word "come."

5. As soon as your dog gets to you, immediately mark the behavior with the word "yes" and give the treat. Repeat this process. Note: Even if you do not have a treat to give your dog every time, still praise him for coming when called. This way, he will always associate coming when called with something positive.

Teaching the "Sit" Command

1. First, find a high-valued treat—something that your dog really loves. To give you a good hint, most dogs love hot dogs. I always use the chicken or turkey hot dogs just because they are healthier.

2. Create a distraction-free environment for your dog (no TV, no kids running around, no other pets around, etc.). Start charging your marker as described earlier. Say your dog's name. When he looks at you, give the verbal marker "yes" and immediately give a treat. This will help get your dog in training mode.

3. Put a treat close to your dog's nose.

4. Move the treat up over your dog's head, as if you were pushing it between their ears, and lure your dog into the sit position as you repeat the command "sit."

5. As soon as your dog is in the sit position, very quickly mark the behavior with a "yes" and give your dog the treat. Repeat process three to five times until your dog has mastered the sit command.

6. To teach your dog to stay in the sit position until released, put him into the sit position, wait a few seconds, and then mark it with a "yes" and give the treat. Then, wait 10 seconds before you give the marker and the treat. Then 30 seconds, one minute, and so on. If the dog gets up before you give the marker, immediately put him back into the sit position and try again. If you notice he is constantly getting up, you may be trying to progress too fast for them. Shorten the time you make them sit before you give the marker, then build the time back up again.

7. Once the dog has mastered staying in the sit position until the marker is given, have him sit, back a few feet away, then give the marker/treat. Again, as he gets better at it, get further away. This teaches the dog the "extended sit." If he gets up before you give the marker, step into him to block him and put him back into the sit position. Then repeat the drill.

Teaching the "Down" Command

1. First, find a high-valued treat—something that your dog really loves. To give you a good hint, most dogs love hot dogs. I always use the chicken or turkey hot dogs just because they are healthier.

2. Create a distraction-free environment for your dog (no TV, no kids running around, no other pets around, etc.). Start charging your marker as described earlier. Say your dog's name. When he looks at you, give the verbal marker "yes" and immediately give a treat. This will help get your dog in training mode.

3. Put a treat close to your dog's nose.

4. Move the treat down to the ground in between his paws. Once your dog goes down, move the treat away from him—pulling it back toward you, but keeping it on the ground.

5. Often, the dog's chest will lower to the ground, but he will keep his hindquarters up in the air. If this happens, push the lure back into your dog until he lies down completely. Then, immediately mark it with "yes" and the treat.

6. To teach your dog to stay in the down position until released, put him into the down position, wait a few seconds, and then mark it with a "yes" and give the treat. Then, wait 10 seconds before you give the marker and treat. Then 30 seconds, one minute, and so on. If he gets up before you give the marker, immediately put him back into the down position and try again. If you notice he is constantly getting up, you may be trying to progress too fast for him. Shorten the time you make him down before you give the marker, then build the time back up again.

7. Once your dog has mastered staying in the down position until the marker is given, you can have him down, back a few feet away, then give the marker and treat. Again, as he gets better at it, get further away. This teaches "extended down." If he gets up before you give the marker, step into him to block him and put him back into the down position. Then repeat the drill.

Alternative Method for Teaching the "Down"

If your dog's hindquarters stay up in the air, or he isn't getting the concept of down, try using your leg to help lure him into the down position. Sit on the floor next to your dog and place the leg that is closest to him flat on the floor. It should be positioned so that your leg is making an arch position or an upside down V beside your dog. Once you have this position, hold the treat under your leg and when your dog goes down to get it, repeat the down command and pull the treat away. He should lower into the down position in order to go under your leg to get the treat. As soon as this happens, mark the behavior with "yes" and reward with treat, then repeat the process.

Teaching the "Stand" Command

1. First, find a high-valued treat—something that your dog really loves. To give you a good hint, most dogs love hot dogs. I always use the chicken or turkey hot dogs just because they are healthier.

2. Create a distraction-free environment for your dog (no TV, no kids running around, no other pets around, etc.). Start charging your marker as described earlier. Say your dog's name. When he looks at you, give the verbal marker "yes" and immediately give a treat. This will help get your dog in training mode.

3. Put your dog into the sit position.

4. With the dog in the sit position, stand facing your dog and put a treat in front of your dog's nose. Slowly pull the treat back toward your chest, luring your dog with the treat to stand up out of the sit position.

5. As you lure your dog toward you, repeat the command "stand." As soon as he gets up out of the sit position and stands up, immediately mark the behavior with "yes" and a reward.

6. To teach your dog to stay in the stand position until released, put him into the stand position, wait a few seconds, then mark it with the "yes" and give the treat. Then, wait 10 seconds before giving the marker and treat. Then 30 seconds, one minute, and so on. If he moves before you give the marker, immediately put him back into the stand position and try again. If you notice he is constantly moving, you may be trying to progress too fast for him. Shorten the time you make him stand before you give the marker, then build the time back up again.

7. Once he has mastered staying in the stand position until the marker is given, you can have him stand, back a few feet away, and give him the marker and treat. Again, as he gets better at it, get further away. This teaches the "extended stand." If he moves before you give the marker, step into him to block him and put him back into the stand position. Then repeat the drill.

Teaching the "Heel" Command

1. First, find a high-valued treat—something that your dog really loves. To give you a good hint, most dogs love hot dogs. I always use the chicken or turkey hot dogs just because they are healthier.

2. Create a distraction-free environment for your dog. I always recommend starting the heel command in a very quiet neighborhood on pavement. The reason we practice on pavement is because there are minimal scent distractions compared to on grass.

3. Have your dog start by sitting on your left side with a leash on.

4. Have a treat in your left hand, step off, and say "heel."

5. Try to keep your dog focused on the treat in your hand, aiming to get him to remain beside you with the treat. Walk approximately 10 feet, stop, have the dog sit, and give the treat. Repeat. As he gets better at it, walk further distances before the treat is given.

Troubleshooting

• If your dog immediately pulls ahead of you, do a 180° turn, putting him back on your left side and try to refocus him on the treat.

• If he gets out of position, have him sit, put him next to your left leg, and start the drill again.

PROS AND CONS OF DIFFERENT TRAINING METHODS

There are several training methods that can be used to train your dog. One of the most common and popular methods is reward-based or treat-based training. This training involves finding something that your dog really likes (ball, hot dogs, treats, tug) and using that as an incentive to get the dog to perform the desired command. The marker and treat training we discussed in the previous chapter is based on this method.

The pro to using this system with a dog who already knows the commands is that you have a dog who is very motivated for the reward. Therefore, they are voluntarily complying with your verbal commands in order to obtain the reward. The benefit of using this method to teach a dog a new command is he is very motivated, focused, and eager to please in order to obtain the reward. Often when using a food reward, the dog will be eager to continue training and learning for long periods of time. Look at it as giving a small kid one small piece of candy at a time every time he or she does something good. It is not enough to get full, but it is enough to make them want more. Another major pro to this system is that anyone can do it with no special knowledge or devices needed. Simply watch a video, grab a pack of hot dogs, and you are all set. That is why this is the most common method of training—any amateur can use this method to train a dog.

Anyone who has used this method for training can tell you that despite its numerous benefits, there are also several problems with it, as well. One of the main complaints with reward-based training is reliability. Remember, this system is based on the dog complying because he wants to get the reward. However, there will come a time when your dog does not want the reward or he is distracted by something more interesting than the reward. At that point, you have lost all obedience because your dog is no longer enticed to perform for the reward. As an example, if you are outside, off-leash with your dog and he spots a squirrel, a bird, or another dog, it will be much more interesting than the treat in your hand. When he is faced with a decision to go for the treat or take off after the squirrel, almost always the "prey" object will win. He will take off running to get the better reward and return when he loses interest in the item that initially distracted him.

The other problem with this system is that there is no consequence for disobedience, meaning, when your dog takes off down the road and will not come back, there is not much you can do in order to give him a consequence for bad behavior. Imagine training a child solely based on positive reinforcement; you get a treat if you do well, you don't get a treat if you misbehave. The child would disobey fairly regularly. Your dog will do the same.

However, reward-based training is fun for you and your dog and it is a cheap, easy, and fast way to start teaching your dog a wide variety of commands with almost no expenses or specialized experience needed. You will be able to teach your dog commands and get decent results with obedience, but you will never have an amazingly obedient dog with this system.

Another popular training method is the prong collar. The prong collar is lined with metal prongs along the interior of the collar. The prong collar is designed to replicate the way the mother would correct her pups in a litter. Or how the alpha-male dog in a pack would correct lower-ranking members of the pack, which is giving a quick nip on the neck. When your dog does not comply with a command, give a quick jerk on the prong collar. Increase intensity of the jerk until your dog complies.

The pro to the prong collar is it is more reliable for obedience than the reward-based system. Using the prong collar, you can still use the reward-based system to motivate the dog, however, now you can use the prong collar to give an instant correction when the dog doesn't listen with the reward-based system. A scenario would be if you had your dog's favorite ball and you tell him to sit. If he doesn't, you give a quick jerk on the prong collar and repeat the command. The prong collar gives him a less than pleasurable feeling and he complies with the command. If he does not comply with the command, increase the intensity of the jerk on the prong collar and repeat the command. This is done until the dog complies. Once he does, give the reward. The dog quickly learns, "If he says sit, I have to do it, so I might as well just do it the first time and get the reward."

In my opinion, there are a few flaws with using the prong collar. One of the biggest is consistency of the correction given, meaning, is your dog being corrected at the same level of correction each day? If you correct your dog with the prong collar, is your correction (jerking on the prong collar) harder or gentler than when your wife corrects your dog with it? Or, when you corrected your dog when he really started to get under your skin, did you correct him much harder than you did yesterday for doing the exact same thing? When it comes to training, there has to be consistency in order for the dog's learning to be maximized.

The second major problem with the prong collar is when your dog is off-leash and away from you. If he is 100 yards away and you call him to come and he doesn't, what do you do? Now, you are back to the same problem you had with the reward-based training—off-leash reliability. Even with the prong collar, neither an instant correction nor a consequence can be given once he is out of your reach.

Overall, prong-collar training is safe, cheap, effective, and very humane when done properly. It is much more effective and reliable than reward-based training, however, it still has a couple of shortfalls.

My preferred method for training dogs is the electronic collar (e-collar). The e-collar comes with a remote control that the owner carries. It is based on almost the same premise as that of the prong collar. It gives a subtle stimulation to the dog's neck area that can be increased in intensity until the dog complies with the command. Modern e-collars are very safe, reliable, and effective when used properly. In fact, almost all police, military, and personal protection dogs are now trained using the e-collar. When using the e-collar, we also use reward-based training for the dog, generally in the form of a toy or praise.

The e-collar has numerous levels of stimulation so its use can be tailored to a specific dogs' temperament and the level of distraction encountered. When the e-collar is used properly, the dog does not view it as a punishment, but views it as a training tool, much like a leash. More important, they actually grow to love it because they associate the e-collar with going outside, off-leash, and having fun. Where other training systems fall short, the e-collar picks up. The range of e-collars vary from 400 yards to two miles. With this system, if your dog is off-leash and you call him to come and he does not, you still can give an instant correction that increases in intensity until he complies with the command.

The e-collar is safe, very effective, and humane when properly used. The shortfalls of the e-collar is that they are much more costly than the other training methods; an average e-collar costs around $200. It is highly recommended that you seek a professional trainer before utilizing this training device. The e-collar can make a disobedient dog perform with amazing precision in a very short time, however, in untrained hands it can completely ruin a dog.

Overall, when choosing a training method for your dog, decide what is most important to you—cost, functionality, or reliability. Whatever method you choose, keep in mind that practice, patience, and consistency are important to achieve great results using any method.

THE DO'S AND DON'TS OF TRAINING

Regardless of what method you choose to train your dog, one of the biggest things you do not want to do is to over-train. Always end your training sessions when the dog is still having fun and is actively engaged in the training. Again, you want to make this a fun process, not a dreaded one. This is especially important with puppies. Everyone wants to get their new puppies trained as rapidly as possible, however, they lose focus of the fact that they are only two or three months old and have an extremely short attention span. If you find yourself chasing your puppy or dog around in order to get it to participate in training, the training session was probably too long and he has completely lost interest. As a general rule, 10-week-old puppies can take about 10 minutes of training at a time; five-month-old puppies can do about 45 minutes at a time. Remember, always end training when the dog wants to keep going, to build up the drive to train.

Once your dog knows the command, never reward him for anything less than exactly what you wanted him to. In training, we see this happen with owners and dogs all too often and it can quickly turn an amazing obedience dog into a marginal one if it continues. For example, if you give the command "down" and your dog almost lies down but is still hovering slightly above the floor and you reward that, he will learn that he does not have to go all the way down in order to get rewarded. By doing this, your dog learns, "Why go all the way down if I can go halfway and get rewarded? I can do half the job and still get the reward." I always tell my clients, "Never reward them once for something you wouldn't want them to do the next 10 times." Dogs are creatures of habit, and they learn amazingly well through repetition. If you reward them once for something, they will try that same thing the next 10 times, especially if it requires less work. So, never reward them for something you wouldn't want them to always do. If they mess up the command or don't do it all the way, make them finish it or just start again from the beginning, but do not reward them unless you want the behavior to be repeated.

Don't be too quick to incorporate distractions while training your dog. I have found that people find this hardest to accept when we start training their dog at our facility. Their dog will have just finished the first lesson and the owner will ask, "Should we start practicing this with a lot of distractions?" No. Your dog has to be amazing at the commands without distractions before they will be *great* with distractions. If your dog is mediocre at a command when it is just the two of you practicing, you can expect nothing but less than mediocre with multiple distractions. It is important to have your dog nearly flawlessly obedient before you start to incorporate distractions. Once he is to the point of near perfection, the distractions should be incorporated slowly. Meaning, do not take them to the middle of the dog park and practice as their first test run with distractions. Start with one other dog around, then two dogs with a couple of people, and then build up from there. By ensuring they are near perfection and then building them up to multiple distractions, you are setting them up for success.

Do not make your sessions obedience training with play built in; try to make them play with obedience built in. What's the difference? Your mindset. When working with your dog, think of it as playing with him and throwing obedience into the play. If you think of it this way, and act this way, then your dog will think the same thing. Dogs are like people— they are much more motivated to learn if they want to do something versus if they feel like they *have* to do something. If you take them out with the intention of making them work on obedience, then they will feel like it is work and will not be as receptive nor motivated. However, if you are taking them out to play and simply incorporate the obedience into the play, then they will be much more receptive because they are wanting to learn. When you find a good balance of play and training, your dog should not even realize he is training.

Do not get frustrated when working with your dog. I know, it sounds a lot easier than it sometimes is. Remember, if you are properly motivating your dog with whatever drives him (treats, tug, toy, ball, etc.), then he wants to learn! So, if for some reason he just isn't picking it up, it is probably more your fault than his. There is a communication problem, and since you are the only one communicating what needs to happen, it is a problem on your end. If you find yourself getting frustrated, it's probably time to stop training for the time being. Also, this will give you time to stop, calm down, and reevaluate your teaching style and method. Again, dogs are like people—what works for one does not necessarily work for another. So, if you saw a great training method on TV, the Internet, or in a book (even this book) do not be afraid to tailor that to what you find works best for your dog. Do not get tunnel vision and start thinking the method you saw is the only way to achieve the desired result. Only you know what motivates your dog the best.

Constantly try to find new things to teach your dog to do. So many people get so focused on teaching them just the basic commands; those are very boring for your dog once he masters them. As soon as your dog masters one command, move forward and teach something new, then repeat. Many people are in awe of my dog, Duke, because he knows 27 commands in English and some in German. Not to mention, he is not yet three years old. As soon as Duke masters a command, I try to be creative and think of something else to start working on with him, in addition to the commands he already knows. It's a constant learning and practicing process. Think of your dog like a kid in school who didn't just learn addition in math and then was done for the rest of his or her life. One learned the basics, and once those were mastered, moved up to something harder. Just like with us, for your dog, learning should be an ongoing cycle that never ends. Dogs that are always learning are never bored. In fact, dogs love to learn just like people do. It stimulates them mentally and makes them use their brain instead of just lying around, eating, and going out to the restroom.

IMPORTANCE OF PHYSICAL
AND MENTAL EXERCISE

The importance of physical and mental exercise cannot be stressed enough as to what it takes in order to raise a perfect dog. Dogs are like people—they need stimulation, they need to get out, and they need to be challenged both physically and mentally. Dogs who are exercised regularly are much happier and healthier than dogs who are not, and the same can be said for people. I always told my friends, family, and clients that whenever I wrote a book on dog training, I would include in it my favorite quote, so here it is: "If you do not give your dog a job to do, they will become self-employed. A self-employed dog will always cost the owner money." What does that mean? If you do not keep your dog actively employed through a job (obedience, training, games, etc.) or exercise, he will find something to do as an outlet of for excessive energy (chew your carpet, eat your couch, chew your furniture, etc.).

In order to exercise them physically, first keep in perspective what type of dog you have, their needs, and their age. If you have a puppy, you really shouldn't be exercising them at all, no more than a simple short walk. A bulldog requires less physical exercise than a boxer or a Lab. So keep in perspective the age and breed of your dog in order to get a good gauge of adequate exercise requirements. What is sufficient for one breed would be too much for another breed, and what is too much for one breed wouldn't be enough for another breed. Do some research on your particular dog in order to assess what would be sufficient.

It is an unfortunate misconception that, for most dogs, simply taking them for a leisurely walk once or twice per day is enough. Often people say, "I walk them twice a day, I don't understand why they still have all this excess energy." Even if you have a dog that is not super high-energy like a boxer or a Malinois, it generally is still not enough to simply walk him. Think about it—you are taking a dog who is born to run for a walk at your pace (which is even slower than the dog's walking pace), and restricting him to a six- to eight-foot leash while doing so. That is not considered "exercise" to a dog. Do you consider it exercise when you are walking in the mall next to a four-year-old with very short strides? I highly doubt it. However, if you were outside for 30 minutes or more, running around non-stop, catching the ball, and running back and forth, you would get pretty worn out. Again, dogs are just like people, if it wouldn't be enough to wear you out, it definitely is not enough to wear out your four-legged friend.

I always encourage my clients to take their dogs to an open field near their house, so their dogs can run around off-leash and chase the ball (for which you have built up their drive). Another good place to take your dog for some off-leash freedom is to a school on weekends because generally nobody is there. Not only can you let them run off-leash, but playgrounds generally have some pretty good fixtures to which you can expose your dog (as discussed in the confidence-building section of this book). Obviously, in order for you to be able to have your dog off-leash, you have to have some form of control over him so you can recall him as needed without the fear of him running off (more on this in the training section).

Another good way to get out some excess energy if you cannot yet trust your dog off-leash, it's cold out, or you do not have time to take him to a park is by the use of a treadmill. Start him off on a low incline at low speeds and at a short distance, then build upon this. Again, only you can decide what would be good for your specific dog. When you put your dog on a treadmill, you can wrap the leash around the hand grips of the treadmill. That way he has enough slack so that it is not pulling on his neck, but there is not enough slack to allow jumping off. Generally, after about a week or two, your dog will start to love the treadmill. When using the treadmill, always supervise your dog while he is using it.

One of the best ways to tire out your dog is through mental stimulation, which works much faster than any form of physical stimulation you could impress upon your dog. Our police and military K9s can run all day, however, if we do a solid hour of obedience or some other form of training with them, they are pretty worn out. Again, comparing dogs to people, what tires you more, walking one or two miles or doing complex math problems for one to two hours straight? With the math problems, your head hurts, you feel drained, you just want to put down the books and shut your eyes. That's how mental stimulation works with dogs, as well. Constant thinking creates a lot of mental stimulation, which tires the entire body.

One of the most basic things you can do to keep your dog mentally stimulated is to practice obedience with him or her—not only practice stuff already mastered, but find new things to teach. Learning completely new concepts will really wear out your dog fast.

Another fun thing you can do is make your dog really use his nose. Place three shoeboxes on the floor and hide a treat under one of them. Make your dog sniff out the one with the treat. Once he is sniffing on the right box, make him sit, then lift the box and reward with the treat. This will teach your dog to use his nose. Soon he will sit on his own once he finds where the treat is hidden. Start throwing in a keyword phrase such as "find the treat." As your dog gets better and better at this game, make it more complex by adding more boxes, different locations, and different treats.

One of the best ways we wear out our dogs is by playing what we refer to as the Tug Game. If your dog is motivated to play tug, we will get the tug and combine obedience with playing tug. We will have them down, sit, heel, etc., then give a verbal marker (as discussed in the marker section of this book) such as "Yes," and activate playing the Tug Game. Meaning, we will play tug with them for approximately 15 or 20 seconds, have them "out" the tug, give one or two more obedience commands, and once they complete them, we will give another verbal marker that engages the the Tug Game. We will repeat this for about 15 minutes. Doing this combines mental stimulation (obedience training) with physical stimulation (the Tug Game). By combining both forms of stimulation, you really wear down your dog much faster. Keep in mind, you always want to end the Tug Game when he still wants to play more (again, build up that drive). Never end because the dog has given up and no longer wants to play, which indicates an over-trained dog.

Remember, anything can be taught to your dog as a game; you do not have to *find* training ways to teach, just make them up as you go. You can put a treat in one hand but display both hands in a fist to your dog and try to make them sniff out which hand holds the treat. Take a couple pairs of old shoes and line them up, putting a treat in one of them, and make your dog find which shoe it's in. These types of drills really make the dogs use their senses extra hard, which is good not only for scent development, but it is good for mental stimulation, as well. Not to mention, it's a fun game for you and your dog and you will bond while playing it. There are no limits to the things you can come up with to keep your dog stimulated. Also, it keeps you stimulated by making you think of new, fun, and creative things to do.

IT CANNOT BE STRESSED ENOUGH THAT IN ORDER TO HAVE A HAPPY DOG, THERE MUST BE MENTAL AND PHYSICAL STIMULATION INVOLVED; IT'S THE *AMOUNT* OF STIMULATION THAT YOU MUST DECIDE.

TROUBLESHOOTING COMMON PROBLEMS

Now we are going to discuss some common problems that people often encounter with their dogs. Remember, almost any problem that your dog displays can be corrected if the proper steps are taken. Some of these problems can easily be fixed yourself, but if the problem is more complex, you may want to consult a professional trainer or behavioral expert.

Nipping is a problem that many people face with their puppies. It has nothing to do with aggression; it is simply them playing with you or if you have a herding breed of dog, it is in their instinct to do this. Even though they are puppies, nips can still be painful and annoying, especially to small children. Nipping is also a way that puppies play and interact with their litter mates. Remember, dogs do not have hands, so their only way to play is by using their mouths. However, now that they have a human family, they must be taught that it is no longer acceptable to play this way.

When a puppy is playing with a litter mate and nips him too hard, the other litter mate will let out a quick yelp and usually walk away, essentially telling the offending dog, "You played too rough, now I am done playing with you." Or, if it gets too rough, often the mother will step in as well and put an end to it. This is how dogs learn what is acceptable play and what is unacceptable—again, the same way that kids learn. When the older brother does something to hurt his little sister, mom steps in, gives a consequence and the older brother learns what he did was too rough.

So if you get a dog that starts nipping, the first thing to try is saying "off" and if he persists, let out a little yelp and simply end the play session. Essentially, you are replicating the same thing that would happen if your dog were with his litter mates. If your dog persistently tries to nip at you, simply isolate him from the family for a few minutes. This becomes your dog's equivalent of a timeout.

Another method that people find very effective is using a bitter-tasting spray, various brands of which are out on the market. This is a liquid with a horribly bitter taste that comes in a spray-style bottle. When your dog nips or chews on something he is not supposed to, repeat the command "off" and if he continues, simply squirt the liquid into his mouth. By doing this, your dog will learn that if he hears "off" and continues his behavior, he will soon have this horrible tasting product in his mouth.

Many people soon realize that having a puppy is much like having a baby; they are a handful and they get into everything and put anything in their mouths—socks, shoes, remote control, keys, cords, and any other fun new "toy" they can find lying around the house. This is a great opportunity to teach them the "out" command, for which you will find a great use over the course of your dog's life. Teaching puppies the "out" command requires him to wear a standard flat collar (not a pinch, choke, or e-collar). As soon as your puppy gets something in his mouth that he shouldn't have, give the command "out." If he does not drop it, pick him up off of the ground by the collar (so the front paws are off the ground) and repeat the word "out." As soon as he drops it, praise him and then try to give him something he can have (a toy, bone, etc.). Picking up and holding the puppy by the collar cuts off the air supply, so the puppy learns, "I can drop this object or run out of air." I can assure you he will drop the object every time. So he begins to associate the word "out" with dropping whatever is in his mouth on command. The reason we try to replace the object with a toy is to teach them, "You cannot have that, but you can have this." Not only does this teach the "out" command, but it also begins to teach the dog what is his.

Destroying things in your home when you are not there. Once you have the nipping, chewing on objects, and outing objects while you are home under control, the next problem may be your dog chewing or destroying things in your home while you are gone. One of the main causes of this problem is simply leaving your dog unsupervised before he is mentally capable of handling the responsibility. If your dog is only six or seven months old, he is about the mental equivalent of a four-year-old child. So, ask yourself, "What would happen if I left my four-year-old out in the house while I went to work?" Likely, the same thing that happens when you leave your dog out—he would find things and destroy them. So, if you leave your dog out, and every day you come home to find things have been ruined, you may want to consider crating your dog until he is older.

Generally, we find that most dogs do well enough to be left unattended in the house at about 18 months of age. At that age, he has the mental capability to handle the responsibility. Additionally, he has had a year and a half of you correcting him when he chews on something that isn't his. So, by this time, he has learned what toys are his and what things are yours. Again, this is a generalization based on working with hundreds of dogs and clients. Therefore, your dog may need more or less time than this.

Once you feel your dog is able to be in the house unsupervised, start this process in small time increments and by giving limited access of the house to your dog. Do not just leave him out with free rein of the house for an entire eight hours. Start by giving him access just to a bedroom for 20 to 30 minutes, and if he does well, expand that time. As he is left alone longer and longer with no incidents, expand the roaming space, meaning, take it from a bedroom to an entire floor. Slowly work up to giving him the entire house. Once taking this step, many people then just keep all bedroom doors shut, essentially leaving the dog to roam freely in the living room, kitchen, and hallway. Doing this will drastically eliminate problems, especially if you have children with toys in their rooms. So, just like with all of the training, start off in small times and spaces, then slowly increase both as your dog gets better and your confidence in him or her increases.

As I touched on at the beginning of this book, the second common cause of a dog destroying things in the house is lack of exercise and stimulation. Remember, "If you do not give your dog a job to do, they will become self-employed. A self-employed dog will always cost the owner money." When a dog does not get exercised regularly or have some form of mental stimulation through obedience or games, he looks for things on which to take out his excess energy. One great way for dogs to burn energy is through running or chewing, which is what they are doing when they lie down and chew on a bone until it disappears. So when your dog has excess energy built up and you are away, he will look for things to chew. If nothing is available, he will chew walls, couches, chair legs, etc. Keep in mind, your dog is not chewing the couch to sabotage you and ruin your life, he just sees it as something to chew on for entertainment.

To prevent your dog from becoming a self-employed dog, ensure he is getting plenty of exercise. Remember, one or two walks per day is not sufficient exercise for most high-energy dogs. They need a lot of mental stimulation or a lot of exercise, meaning, off-leash, running around, with a lot of open-space exercise. Mental and physical stimulation will fully benefit you and your dog.

If you follow the guidance on using the crate and providing your dog with daily physical and mental stimulation, you will almost completely eliminate the problem of things in your home being chewed on or destroyed by the new member of your family.

Separation anxiety is when your dog becomes very saddened or depressed when left alone. Some common symptoms of separation anxiety is your dog destroying things in the house; relieving himself in the house when you are away; excessive barking, pacing, and panting when he knows you are about to leave; and breaking out of his crate.

Separation anxiety can be caused by numerous things. Dogs are very social creatures to begin with. Constantly being with a "pack" is just in their nature. Dogs are descendants of wolves, which are always in a pack. Wolves know they need to be in a pack to survive. Therefore, they are very rarely alone. Separation anxiety is more prevalent in some breeds than in others. For example, shepherds, Malinois, and collies are more likely to have separation anxiety than a breed such as a pug. Separation anxiety is somewhat common in shelter or rescue dogs, as well. These dogs can develop separation anxiety when they are adopted by a new family. While in the shelter or rescue, they are always around other dogs and people. When they go to a new family and routine, they may be in their crate or left alone for eight hours while the family goes to work or school.

So the dog goes from constantly being with people and animals to being left alone. This can create separation anxiety.

Separation anxiety can also be caused by the dog being taken from its mother too early; it may not have developed the social bonds that a puppy normally would. Puppies removed from their mother and siblings too early are more likely to develop separation anxiety and excessive barking problems. That is why it is essential to find a good breeder who will not give puppies away until they are at least eight weeks old.

Lastly, a major change in the dog's routine can cause separation anxiety. For example, if it is summertime and you or your children are home a lot or you go on a long vacation together, your dog gets adapted to being with the pack every day for a prolonged period of time. If suddenly your routine changes—you go back to work and the kids go back to school— your dog suddenly finds himself home alone every day, causing him separation anxiety.

There are numerous things you can do to drastically curb this separation anxiety behavior and ultimately eliminate it. First off, never punish your dog for this behavior. Remember, they are exhibiting this behavior because they miss you so much. Obviously, you never punish a dog because he misses you and does not know how to act when you're not around.

One of the main things you can do to help is providing more separation, meaning, make the dog spend more time alone. Do not let him be so clingy when you are home with him. If you have a fenced-in backyard, make him go out and stay out there for short periods of time. If you are home, put him in a separate room or in his crate throughout the day. While he is separated from you (in a different room or crate) give him his favorite toy or treat, so he starts associating being separated from you as getting a reward and it gives him something to do other than thinking about you. Again, never let him out of the room or crate while he is barking or whining—this will teach him that barking or whining will get him out. Wait for him to be calm and quiet, go to him, praise him, and let him come back to the family. That way, he gets used to being separated when you are there, which slowly makes the separation when you are gone much easier.

When leaving the house., try not to make a big deal out of it. When you put the dog in the crate or are leaving the house, try to be emotionless—do not squat down and overly pet him while talking cute: "Oh baby, we are going to miss you," etc. Just get ready and leave the house without acknowledging the dog. If you make a big deal out of leaving, the dog, too, will see it as a big deal. The same principle applies when returning home—be emotionless. Do not open the door, rush over and pet the dog, and tell him how much you missed him. When you go, leave out toys and something that has your scent on it (an old unwashed shirt, for example). That way, he will have something that smells like you. This has been known to really help calm down a dog.

Another thing I always recommend doing is filling a Kong with peanut butter and putting in the freezer. When you are ready to leave, put the Kong out for the dog. This serves two purposes: It gives him something to do and work on and it gives him a treat when you leave (again, associating you leaving with a good thing). Also, leave the television or a radio on so the dog still hears people's voices, creating the illusion that there are still people around.

Lastly, if you have the time and money, you can always hire a midday dog walker or take the dog to a doggy day care before you leave for work. This will give him more time with people and less time alone. However, it should be noted that this does not cure separation anxiety; it just prevents it. Meaning, it's a short-term solution to a long-term problem.

Overall, if your dog develops or already has separation anxiety, the best cure is more time apart and even more separation. Again, it's important to do more separation while you are home. Start in small increments and then slowly increase until your dog gets used to being apart from you. Make the separation as positive an experience as possible and use the techniques listed above. If the separation anxiety continues to worsen, contact a trained professional.

Excessive barking is a problem many people face with their dog regardless of breed, age, or size. It can result from a number of things. Like with separation anxiety, some dogs such as hounds, shepherds, and Labs are naturally more vocal than some of the other breeds. Shepherds are protective dogs, therefore, they will bark at someone knocking on the door, a noise outside, or someone walking by the house. Labs, like shepherds, are very prey-driven dogs. Therefore, if they see a squirrel or a cat outside, often they will bark excessively. Boredom and a lack of exercise can also contribute to excessive barking.

There are a few things you can do to curb or completely eliminate this behavior. One of the easiest and most immediate fixes is the use of a bark collar. A bark collar is simply a dog collar that has a vibration sensor built into it. When the dog barks, it delivers a subtle electronic stimulation on the neck, and if the barking continues, the stimulation gets more intense until it reaches a very uncomfortable level. The dog will see that every bark is met with an increased stimulation and will begin to associate barking with the electronic stimulation. The dog will simply quit barking to avoid the stimulation. The great thing about bark collars is that they work almost immediately.

Also, it does not teach your dog not to bark, it simply teaches him not to bark while the collar is on.

Of course, as stated earlier, mental and physical exercises, keeping your dog stimulated, and desensitizing him to noises and objects all will drastically help prevent your dog from barking excessively.

Aggression is one of the most common issues that we deal with at our facility in Virginia, both dog-on-dog aggression and people aggression. As I stated earlier, almost all aggression in dogs stem from a lack of socialization with people and other animals or bad experiences with them (being bitten, beaten, etc.). That is why I cannot stress enough the importance of positive socialization with other people and animals. If your dog becomes dog- or people-aggressive, you will probably isolate him from the thing toward which he is aggressive, when in fact, you need to take the opposite approach. Isolating the dog from the problem will never address the issue. Consult a trainer who can help you deal with the issue and start positively socializing your dog around the people or dogs to whom he is aggressive.

Counter-Surfing is another common problem for dog owners, especially with dogs who have a very high motivation for food. This is when a dog jumps up on the counters or tables in an attempt to grab some food. Obviously, this can be very annoying after you just spent time making dinner; a cake; or something special for a family or friend, only to find that your beloved furry family member has taken the liberty of sampling it for himself.

One of the best ways to stop this is by simply being proactive in prevention. Would you leave a box of candy or bars of ice cream in your five-year-old child's room? I highly doubt it. This is because you know it would be too great of a temptation

71

and they do not yet have the acquired discipline that it takes to refrain from eating. Your puppy or dog has the same mentality. Unless he is older, more mature, or not very food-driven, he, too, will not yet have the discipline to refrain from swiping your delicious food that is sitting just out of reach of his mouth.

Other than being proactive, there is really only one solution, which is to give your dog a consequence for his counter-surfing. This can be done in a couple of ways. If your dog does not have any advanced method of training (electronic collar or prong collar), when you catch him in the act, immediately give a timeout. As soon as you see him going for the food, give a loud "off" and put him in timeout, separating him from the family for a period of time. If your dog is trained with some advanced training method, your trainer can explain how to use that specific device to curb these behaviors.

Submission urination is also a problem that many new dog owners encounter. It is usually seen in puppies or abused dogs. Submissive urination is not necessarily a bad thing, even though it may seem quite annoying when it happens at your house, on your new floors, or on your rug. This is simply a dog's way of showing that he acknowledges you are the boss and he has not yet learned other ways to express this. Puppies will grow out of this behavior, especially with confidence-building drills and obedience training. If you experience this with your adult dog, it is usually due to insecurity and low confidence, which require confidence-building drills and obedience.

Never punish your dog for submissive urination—he does this because of low self–confidence, so punishment will only escalate the problem. Essentially, do nothing to your dog, meaning neither punish nor praise him. Petting him teaches that it's a good thing (because he is praised for it). If you pet your dog and he urinates, immediately stop petting him and walk away.

Excited urination is when your puppy gets so excited by a person, place, or thing that he cannot control his bladder and may piddle a little bit. Again, you cannot punish him for this. Often puppies are so excited they do not even realize what they've done. So, if you punish them, excited urination can turn into submissive urination.

A common scenario that causes excited urination is when your dog is home, someone walks in the door, and immediately greets the dog. The dog starts to learn that when the door opens and someone walks in, he is immediately played with and has fun. Often when the door opens, the dog gets really excited and as soon as the person entering touches the dog, he will urinate excitedly.

One of the best ways to prevent or help cure this is by socializing and noise/object-desensitization drills as discussed earlier. Even if you do all of these things flawlessly, there is still a good chance your young puppy at some point will display excited urination. Another thing that works quite well is to have the people who walk in pay absolutely no attention to your dog for a few minutes or until he is completely calm. This teaches your dog that the door opening or someone walking in means absolutely nothing and he gets nothing out of it, so he has no reason to be excited. Another good trick is to make your dog go into a sit or down position before you praise him. Generally, dogs will not piddle if they are in the sit or down position, which make them contain their excitement in an obedience position. So, walk in, make your dog sit, and when he does, pet him. If he gets up from the sit position, immediately stop praising him and make him sit again before the praise continues. This alone will almost completely eliminate the excited urination.

Digging can be annoying, expensive, and quite frustrating when you have a nicely groomed backyard. There are numerous reasons that dogs dig up the backyard, however, the main reason is boredom. Notice that seems to be a common theme in this book? Remember: "A bored dog is a destructive dog." When your dog is bored or unexercised, digging is a great outlet of energy. When I tell my clients this, many of them say something such as, "I don't see why how he is bored or doen't get exercise, we have a whole acre in our backyard." I always respond to them with this question: "You have a big neighborhood, correct? Well how do you get bored when you can go anywhere in your neighborhood?" Even though you may have a big backyard, it is the same backyard your dog has been in his whole life. It's the same smells and the same sights, so now he is bored with it and will look for other things to do for entertainment.

Your dog needs to be in new environments and needs mental and physical stimulation regardless of how big your yard is. Another reason dogs dig is they are literally trying to break out and go into a new territory. Have you noticed your dog has tried to dig under the fence? Again, he is bored with the big backyard so he tries to get out and find new things to look at, smell, and taste. If you constantly take him out to new environments, then being out will lose its appeal because it's nothing new to him. Another reason he could be digging to escape is if there is a female in heat nearby; he could be digging to get to the other dog to mate. The only way to eliminate this is by neutering or spaying your dog.

Dogs are great savers; they will bury their bones or treats for another day if they do not immediately want them. An easy way to prevent this is to not let your dog take his bones outside of the house. If you are letting your dog in the backyard, ensure that he is not taking anything out there with him. That way, he won't have any bones or food to bury.

If your dog is not burying anything, not trying to escape by the fence, and is getting plenty of physical and mental stimulation throughout the day, the problem may be the heat. Dogs quickly learn that it is cooler just beneath the surface of the ground, so they may dig up a nice cool spot to lie on. A very simple way to eliminate this is provide them with a cool and shaded area. Preferably have something to lie on that is elevated from the hot ground. There are many dog beds on the market that are elevated a few inches above the ground and made with mesh-type fabric so the cool air circulates underneath. These work, are cheap, last a long time, dogs love them, and they will prevent your dog from digging for a cool spot.

Some of the other reasons your dog could be digging are for small game in your backyard or if you are using any form of bone or blood meal to fertilize your garden. These can create an irresistible scent for your dog that makes him dig to uncover a bone he thinks is there.

If none of the above methods work, there are commercial products that can be applied directly to plants and grass. These products give off a repugnant scent that interferes with the dog's scent (only temporarily). These products also work great on nuisance animals, as well. This is the easiest solution if you have a specific area that is being dug up constantly.

Jumping on people is another common problem that can be easily corrected with advanced training (with an electronic or prong collar). However, if you do not want to use one of these methods or your puppy is too young to be trained using these methods, there are still a few things you can do to curb this behavior. Also know that your puppy isn't trying to sabotage your life and get his muddy paw prints all over your new shirt. In fact, it's usually quite the opposite. Generally dogs jump on people because they really like them and are seeking affection or play. I know, that still doesn't make you feel better about the situation.

A good solution is to simply not pay any attention to the dog whatsoever. I know that's easier said than done, however, if you have the patience to try this method and see it through, it usually works quite well. Generally dogs jump to try to engage you and elicit a response. Therefore, if you stand there, arms folded, and do not acknowledge him in any way, he will soon find that you are rather boring. If that method doesn't seem to work, try putting your knee into his chest every time he goes to jump on you. This will quickly teach the dog that, "Every time I jump, I get an unpleasant feeling in my chest." A final method is simply getting him trained in obedience. He learns that jumping gets him nowhere and sitting gets them praised and/or treats.

Never praise your dog when he jumps on you. Doing so teaches him that if he jumps up on someone enough, that person will ultimately pet him. So again, you are rewarding a bad behavior. Also, you will probably find that simply pushing him off may make the problem worse. Pushing them off turns into a game for many dogs. They think, "I jump, you push, I jump again, repeat. Wow, this is fun."

SUMMARY

If you follow all the guidance in this book, I can assure you that you will have a highly confident, friendly, and well-trained dog. Remember, dogs are animals; they are not kids and should not be treated like kids. Although they are members of the family, they have to learn their place in the family. Their place in the family should always be at the bottom of the pack. If you treat your dog as an equal to the family members, you create problems. Dogs are pack animals; they have to know their place in your pack. Even though you may see him as an equal, your dog will not see himself this way. He will try to figure out where he is in your pack. So you must make it known through doing all of these steps that he is at the bottom of the pack.

I hope you use all the tools and information in this book in order to raise the perfect dog.

ABOUT THE AUTHOR

Nicholas grew up in the small country town of Urbana, Ohio. Upon graduating from high school, he immediately joined the U.S. Marine Corps. During his time in the Marine Corps, he was stationed at Camp Pendleton, California. He also lived in Okinawa, Japan, and spent seven months in Fallujah, Iraq, where his unit was the first to go into the city for seven long months of combat operations. Nicholas received the Navy and Marine Corps Commendation Medal for his heroic actions in Fallujah. After getting out of the Marine Corps, he was hired to do executive protection for one of the most well-known celebrities in the country. After a few years of this, he was hired by a federal law enforcement agency doing executive protection. Now, Nicholas resides in Woodbridge, Virginia, where he works as a consultant for the government and operates his highly successful dog-training business.

Made in the USA
Middletown, DE
27 January 2017